COOKING with WINE

HEARTS 'N TUMMIES COOKBOOK COMPANY
A Dinky Division of Quixote Press
1854-345th Avenue
Wever IA   52658
1-800-571-2665

To wine lovers everywhere - I hope you enjoy these recipes as much as we do!

TABLE OF CONTENTS

5

Nowadays there are vineyards springing up from coast to coast, north to south. In places you would never dream they would be. In the desert, on mountains, on the plains. All have a variety of grapes from the region and have a flavor of their own.

Being a wine lover for many years, not a connoisseur, you understand just enjoying good wine from various regions, I have collected recipes from many places and friends. I love to cook with wine and there is nothing like the flavor wine brings out in the food.

There are many wine festivals spring through fall and it's wonderful to go to different regions and taste the special grapes of the area.

The following list is just a sample of wines that can be used for drinking and cooking. Go to a reputable wine shop or, better yet, a vineyard and talk with the vintner. They know their wines and can make suggestions.

The recipes included in this little book are either out of my own kitchen or from friends who have been cooking with wine for years. Hope you enjoy them.

WINE GUIDE

Type	Temperature	Serve With
Appetizer Wines		
Dry Sherry	Room temperature	Appetizers
Flavored Wines	or chilled to about	
Vermouth (sweet	50°	
or dry)		

Dinner Wines

Burgundy (red)	**Room temperature**	
Claret		
Merlot		Beef, veal, pork, game, pasta, eggs
Cabernet Sauvignon		
Rosé	**Chilled to 50°**	

Chablis (white)	**Chilled to 50°**	
Chardonnay		Fish, poultry,
Riesling		
Gewürztraminer		
Sauterne		ham
Rhine		

9

Dessert Wines
Tawny Port   **Room temperature**
Cream Sherry
Sauterne (sweet)
Tokay
Madeira

Sparkling Wines
Champagne   **Chilled to 50°**
Spumante
Sparkling Burgundy
Sparkling Rosé

Desserts fruit and cheese

All occasions

10

WINE NOTES

White wines are more acidic than others and chilling takes away from the sharp taste, mellowing them. Best served at about 50 degrees. Red wines should be served room temperature. Best served at 70 degrees. It is best to drink table wines within a day or two . These can be kept if refrigerated and tightly corked for up to a week.

Sparkling wines should be chilled as the white wines are, as it slows down the escaping of the bubbles. Chill about 3 hours. These wines will go flat after a period of time after being opened. They can be used for cooking when they go flat. 11 (more)

(continued)

Dessert wines are usually served with dessert and should be cool. They are a fruity wine, high in alcohol content and are best kept cool between uses. These wines should be treated in the same way as table wines.

USING WINE IN COOKING

Using wine in cooking is for flavor and aroma not alcohol content. It's a subtle flavor, just a hint, not the main ingredient.

When heating wine take care to not overheat as the flavor will all burn off. It begins evaporating relatively soon, much sooner than water.   The flavors change as it heats. If it is barely heated it will retain most of its flavor, but if its boiled or cooked for a long time its flavors evaporate.

If it is cooked over high heat it reduces and the flavor concentrates. The liquid evaporates and the flavor increases.

SUGGESTIONS FOR USING WINE

- Use wine to give foods a different flavor.
- Add directly to foods, pour over fruit or ice cream.
- Useful as a tenderizer. It gives food a wonderful flavor.
- Use as a poaching liquid or for simmering meats.
- Good for marinating liquids.
- Use the same type of wine in cooking as you would with the dish.
- Cooking wines are not for drinking and are not necessarily useful for cooking. Use a bottle of wine instead.

15

NOTES;

SOUPS

SOUPS

Carrot Soup...19-20
Cream of Pecan Soup...21-22
Creamy Mushroom Soup...23-24
Gazpacho...25-26
Onion Soup (for crockpot)...27-28
Seafood Chowder with White Wine...29-30
Wild Rice Soup with Sherry...31-32
Zucchini Soup with White Wine...33-34
Squash Soup...35

CARROT SOUP

1 c. onions, chopped	1 T. coriander
4 T. butter or margarine	4 c. chicken broth
1/2 c. white wine	salt and pepper to taste
1 lb. carrots, minced	

Sauté onion in butter or margarine until soft. Add wine and carrots and cover tightly. Simmer for about 30 minutes, stirring occasionally.

Put mixture in blender or food processor with some of

19   **(more)**

(continued)
the chicken broth and blend until smooth. Return to
pan and whisk in remaining broth and salt and pepper.
Serve warm.

CREAM OF PECAN SOUP

1-1/2 T. butter or margarine   3 c. chicken broth
3-1/2 c. onion, minced   salt to taste
6 T. tomato sauce   1/3 c. heavy cream
3/4 c. pecans, ground to a   1 tsp. nutmeg
    paste   1 c. red wine

Melt butter or margarine over medium heat and add
the onion and cook, stirring often until soft. Add
tomato sauce and continue cooking for 2 minutes.

                                             (more)

(continued)
Add the pecan paste and stir it into the onion mixture.
Whisk in the broth a little at a time, making sure each
addition is well incorporated before adding more.

Add wine and bring to a boil then turn down heat and
simmer for 10 minutes. Salt to taste and add the cream
and simmer until warmed through. Serve with a
sprinkle of nutmeg.

CREAMY MUSHROOM SOUP

1/4 c. bacon, chopped
2 T. olive oil
1/2 c. onions, diced
1/2 c. carrots, diced
1/2 c. celery, diced
3 c. mushrooms, sliced
1 c. burgundy

1 clove garlic, minced
1 c. potatoes, diced
4 c. chicken broth
2 c. water
1/4 c. heavy cream
1 T. lemon juice

In large pot, cook bacon over medium heat until almost crisp. Add olive oil, onions, carrots, celery, mushrooms,

23   **(more)**

(continued)

garlic and potatoes. Cover and cook the mixture over low heat for about 8 minutes until vegetables are soft. Add broth and water and bring to a boil. Reduce heat and simmer about 15 minutes, until potatoes are cooked.

Strain soup, reserving broth. Put vegetables in a food processor or blender and add 1/2 c. broth and puree until smooth. Add pureed liquid and burgundy to remaining broth and bring to a simmer. Turn off heat and stir in cream and lemon juice. Season to taste.

GAZPACHO

1/2 c. white wine
1 T. olive oil
1 sm. red onion, quartered
1 sm. green pepper, seeded
  cut up

1/2 cucumber, peeled and
  chopped
2 tomatoes, peeled, seeded
  and chopped
2 c. tomato juice

In a blender or food processor, put wine, oil, onion, green pepper and cucumber. Blend until smooth. Add tomatoes and blend until just finely chopped. Stir in tomato juice. Chill and serve.

(more)

(continued)

Garnish with thin slices of unpeeled cucumber, sliced green pepper, red onions, or crusty croutons. A great summer soup.

ONION SOUP
(For Crockpot)

1 qt. beef broth	1 c. Parmesan cheese
3 c. onions, thinly sliced	1 tsp. salt
1/4 c. sugar	2 T. flour
1/4 c. butter or margarine	1 c. red wine

Put broth in crockpot and cover. Set on high. Cook onions in a large skillet in butter or margarine. Cover

(more)

(continued)
and cook about 15 minutes. Uncover and add salt,
sugar and flour, stir well. Add to broth in crockpot.
Cover and cook on low 6 to 8 hours or on high 3 hours.
About 1 hour before serving, add wine.

Serve with grated Parmesan cheese.

SEAFOOD CHOWDER WITH WHITE WINE

1 sm. onion, chopped
1 clove garlic, minced
1 stalk celery, chopped
1 sm. carrot, chopped
olive oil
1/4 tsp. ea. basil and oregano

2 c. chicken broth
1 c. white wine
1/2 lb. shrimp or scallops
cooked rice
salt and pepper to taste

Sauté vegetable lightly in olive oil. Add 2 c. broth and seasonings. Simmer 15 minutes. Add seafood and wine and cook 10 minutes longer. Serve over rice.

29   (more)

(continued)

For a variation of this recipe, add peeled, chopped tomatoes when adding the broth.

WILD RICE SOUP WITH SHERRY

5 T. butter or margarine   3 T. pecans, finely chopped
3 T. green onions, chopped   salt and pepper to taste
1/2 c. flour   4 T. dry sherry
3 C. chicken broth   1 c. half and half
2 C. wild rice, cooked   parsley for garnish
1/2 c. cooked ham, cubed
1/4 c. carrots, finely grated

Melt butter or margarine in a large saucepan and sauté
(more)

(continued)

onions. Blend in flour and gradually add the broth.
Cook, stirring constantly until the mixture comes to a
boil. Cook for 1 minute. Stir in the rice, ham, carrots,
pecans, salt and pepper and simmer for 5 minutes.

Add the half and half and sherry and stir until blended.
Heat until warm, *but do not boil.* Garnish with parsley
and serve.

ZUCCHINI SOUP WITH WHITE WINE

4 slices bacon, cooked   1/2 c. white wine
1 med. onion, chopped   2 T. parsley
1 clove garlic, minced   1 tsp. basil
1 10-1/2 oz. can beef broth   pepper to taste
2-1/2 c. water   8 med. zucchini, sliced
Parmesan cheese   thinly

In bacon drippings, sauté onions and garlic. Add
remaining ingredients except Parmesan cheese. Simmer
uncovered until zucchini is tender, about 15 minutes.

(more)

(continued)
Let cool then put in blender or food processor and
blend until smooth.

Reheat and serve with Parmesan cheese sprinkled on
top.

This freezes extremely well.

SQUASH SOUP

2 lbs. yellow squash   1 med. onion, chopped
2 cans chicken broth   1 8 oz. pkg. cream cheese
1/2 c. wine   salt and pepper to taste

Cut squash into small pieces and combine with onion in chicken broth. Cook until tender.

In a blender or food processor combine 1/2 squash mixture and 1/2 cream cheese. Puree until smooth. Repeat for balance. Return to pot, add the wine and simmer for 15 minutes. Add salt and pepper to taste.

35

VEGETABLES

VEGETABLES

BAKED MUSHROOMS IN WINE

1 lb. mushrooms, halved
1/4 c. butter or margarine,
   melted
1 T. chives, chopped
1/2 tsp. rosemary

salt and pepper to taste
1/4 c. dry sherry
1/2 c. chicken broth

Combine all ingredients in an ungreased baking dish.
Cover and bake at 350° for 20 minutes.

MUSHROOM AND WINE CASSEROLE

1 lb. fresh mushrooms	1/2 c. chicken broth
1 T. rosemary	1/2 c. dry white wine
1 T. chives, minced	salt and pepper to taste

1/2 c. butter or margarine, melted

Slice mushrooms into a baking dish. Combine butter with rosemary, chives, salt and pepper. Add broth and wine, stir well and pour over mushrooms. Cover and bake at 350° for 20 minutes.

This is wonderful served over a steak or roast beef.

CHABLIS ASPARAGUS

2 lb. fresh asparagus	1/4 tsp. rosemary
1/2 onion, chopped	1/4 tsp. thyme
1/2 c. butter or margarine	1/4 tsp. salt
	1/2 c. Chablis
	parsley for garnish

Cook asparagus to slightly underdone, put spears in a casserole dish. Sauté onions in butter or margarine until soft and tender, not browned. Stir in spices.

(more)

41

(continued)
Remove from heat and spoon over asparagus. Pour in wine and bake at 400° for 5 minutes. Sprinkle with chopped parsley.

This can be made ahead of time but add wine just before cooking.

BURGUNDY MUSHROOMS

1 lb. fresh mushrooms   1/4 c. burgundy
1/2 c. salad oil   1 T. garlic powder

Remove the stems from the mushrooms. Rinse caps and
dry thoroughly. Combine oil, burgundy and garlic
powder. Marinate overnight, stir occasionally.

43

MUSHROOM RICE

1/2 c. rice, cooked
1/2 lb. mushrooms, sliced

2 green onions, chopped
1 T. butter or margarine
1/4 c. dry white wine

While rice is cooking, sauté mushrooms over high heat until golden and liquid is evaporated. Add wine and simmer, stirring occasionally until wine is evaporated. Fluff rice and stir in mushroom mixture and green onions.

MUSHROOM RICE WITH SHERRY

1 clove garlic, minced
1/2 T. butter or margarine
2 c. mushrooms, sliced
1/4 c. red bell pepper,
   chopped
1 c. chicken broth
1/4 c. water

1/4 c. dry sherry
2 tsp. onion, chopped
salt to taste
1-1/2 c. instant rice
2 T. Parmesan cheese,
   grated
1 T. parsley

Cook garlic in butter or margarine about 1 minute.
Add mushrooms and red pepper, stir occasionally about

45

(more)

(continued)
2 minutes. Add broth, water, sherry, onion flakes and salt. Bring to a full boil and stir in rice. Cover and remove from heat. Let stand 5 minutes then fluff rice with a fork. Sprinkle with Parmesan cheese and parsley.

MARINATED MUSHROOMS

8 oz. button mushrooms   1 T. parsley, chopped
white wine   1 bay leaf
Olive oil   3 cloves
1 T. onion, finely chopped   salt and pepper to taste
1 T. chives, finely chopped   dash Tabasco
    1 clove garlic

Put mushrooms in a jar or covered bowl and cover with white wine and let stand overnight in the refrigerator.

(more)

47

(continued)
Drain wine and combine remaining ingredients and pour over mushrooms. Cover again and allow to stand for 2 days in the refrigerator. Drain and serve.

Take the 3 days to make these, it's worthwhile. They have a wonderful flavor.

ONIONS IN WINE

2 T. olive oil
2 cloves garlic, crushed
4 onions, sliced

1 T. Italian spices
1/2 c. white wine
salt and pepper to taste

Heat oil in skillet and add garlic and onions. Sauté until lightly brown. Add spices and wine and simmer about 10 minutes until onions are tender. Salt and pepper to taste.

A good side dish with any meat or fish and also as a relish.

49

RED CABBAGE

2 T. butter or margarine
2 T. sugar
3/4 c. red wine
1 c. water
4 cloves
2 onions, sliced

2 apples, unpeeled and
   cored, cut into wedges
1 head red cabbage,
   cut into quarters
salt and pepper to taste

Melt butter or margarine in a large skillet and add sugar, wine, water and cloves. Stir well then add remaining ingredients. Cover and simmer 2 hours. *This is good with pork or poultry.*

SAUTÉED MUSHROOMS

1-1/2 lb. mushrooms, sliced thinly

1/2 c. butter or margarine
1 c. dry white wine

Melt butter or margarine and add mushrooms. Sauté, stirring occasionally until mushrooms are a deep golden brown and the liquid disappears, 25 minutes. Add wine and cook until it reduces completely.

Serve with grilled steak or chops.

SHERRIED CARROTS

2 lbs. carrots, sliced thinly 1/4 c. cream sherry
2 T. olive oil salt and pepper to taste
parsley for garnish

Sauté carrots in oil until they begin to brown. Add sherry and simmer for about 5 minutes, uncovered, stirring often. Salt and pepper to taste and garnish with parsley.

SHERRIED VEGETABLE DIP

2 3 oz. pkgs. cream cheese   1/8 c. sherry
1/2 c. bleu cheese   1/2 tsp. onion, grated
2 T. butter or margarine

Let cream cheese, bleu cheese and butter or margarine
stand until room temperature. Cream together and add
sherry and onion. Mix well. Chill for several hours
before serving.

Serve with raw vegetables or crudites.

53

SPRING VEGETABLES AND WINE

2 c. carrots, sliced thinly   1 clove garlic, minced
2 c. zucchini, sliced thinly   1 T. lemon juice
2 T. olive oil   3 T. dry white wine

Sauté carrots in oil for 2 minutes then add zucchini.
Toss and cook for 3 more minutes. Add lemon juice
and wine. Remove from heat and toss to coat. Serve
immediately.

SUMMER VEGETABLE CASSEROLE

2 lg. potatoes, thinly sliced	salt and pepper to taste
1 lg. onion, thinly sliced	3/4 c. white wine
2 med. zucchini, chopped	3 T. butter or margarine
4 tomatoes, chopped	1 c. bread crumbs
2 carrots, thinly sliced	2 c. cheddar cheese,
tarragon or other herbs of	grated
choice to taste	

Put vegetables in a baking dish in order given and
season each layer with salt, pepper and herbs. Pour

(more)

(continued)
wine over all and cover and bake 1 hour at 375°.

Melt butter or margarine in a skillet and stir in bread
crumbs until they have absorbed the butter. Sprinkle
cheese over casserole, then bread crumbs and bake
another 15 minutes, uncovered so crumbs brown.

TOMATO MUSHROOM CURRY

1-1/2 c. button mushrooms   1 tsp. curry powder
1 lg. tomato, diced   1/2 tsp. fennel seed
2 T. olive oil   1/4 tsp. ground ginger
1/2 sm. onion, minced   salt to taste
1/2 c. red wine

Heat oil in a large skillet. When oil is hot add onions, spices and salt. Crush the fennel seeds before adding.

(more)

57

(continued)
Stir for 1 minute then add sliced mushrooms and
tomatoes and wine. Stir well so all are coated with
spices. Turn heat to low and simmer for 12-15 minutes,
until mushrooms are cooked through and wine has
reduced.

NOTES:

MAIN DISHES

MAIN DISHES

Pasta

Lamb

Seafood

EGGPLANT AND PASTA

1 eggplant, diced
2 t. salt
1/4 c. olive oil

2 c. spaghetti sauce of
    choice
1 c. red wine
1/2 lb. pasta, cooked

Mix the salt with the diced eggplant and let sit in a colander for 30 minutes. Rinse and pat dry.

In a large skillet, sauté eggplant until browned. Mix
(more)

(continued)
into the spaghetti sauce and cook until tender. Pour
over pasta and sprinkle with grated Romano or
Parmesan cheese.

PASTA WITH MUSHROOM SAUCE

1 T. butter or margarine
1/4 c. olive oil
1 lb. portobello mushrooms
2 cloves garlic
1/4 tsp. red pepper flakes
1 c. chicken broth
1/2 c. red wine
1 chicken bouillon cube
1-1/2 T. parsley
salt to taste
1 lb. tubular pasta of choice
1/4 c. Parmesan, grated

Chop mushrooms into small pieces. Combine butter or margarine and oil in a large skillet and sauté mushrooms. Add garlic and red pepper flakes. Cook over medium heat until liquid from the mushrooms

67

(more)

(continued)
evaporates, about 10 minutes.

Add broth, wine and bouillon cube and increase heat to high and cook 10 minutes to blend and for the liquid to reduce somewhat. Remove from heat and add salt and parsley.

Cook pasta according to package directions and drain completely. Return to pot and add mushroom sauce and stir over medium heat until warm. Remove from heat and add Parmesan cheese and toss to mix.

SPRINGTIME BUTTERFLIES

1 red bell pepper, sliced thinly
1 carrot, julienned
1 zucchini, sliced thinly
4 oz. snow peas, thinly sliced
pinch of sugar
8 oz. butterfly pasta, cooked
1 T. finely grated lemon peel
3 T. olive oil
4 lg. plum tomatoes, cut into 8 pieces
1/2 c. white wine
1 c. basil, torn
2 green onions, chopped
2 t. parsley
salt and pepper to taste

Blanch pepper and carrot strips for 30 seconds in

69

(more)

(continued)

boiling water. Add the zucchini strips and snow peas, cook for 1 minute longer. Drain and rinse under cold water. Pat dry and set aside. Cook pasta according to directions. Drain and set aside. Heat oil over medium heat. Add tomatoes, wine, 1/2 c. basil and the sugar. Cook 3-4 minutes, stirring gently.

Toss in the cooked pasta. Add blanched vegetables, scallions, remaining basil, parsley and lemon zest. Toss well and season with salt and pepper.

LEG OF LAMB WITH WINE

1/4 c. green onions, chopped salt and pepper to taste
1 c. dry sherry 3/4 tsp. garlic powder
leg of lamb juice of 1 lemon
2 T. butter or margarine
1 tsp. oregano

Combine green onions and sherry and pour over lamb.
Marinate overnight, turning once.   Combine butter,
oregano, salt, pepper and garlic powder and spread
over meat.

71 **(more)**

(continued)

Put lamb in an uncovered roasting pan and cook 25 minutes at 425° Lower heat to 300° and pour marinade over lamb adding lemon juice. Cover and cook until tender, 2-3 hours depending on size. Baste often.

When cooked, remove lamb to a platter and mix a small amount of flour and sherry to juices in pan. *Do not make too thick of a gravy, it should be thin with lamb.*

CALIFORNIA FISH STEW

1 T. olive oil
1 clove garlic, minced
1/2 c. onion, chopped
1/3 c. green pepper,
   chopped
1/4 lb. mushrooms, sliced
2 c. tomatoes, cooked
3/4 c. tomato paste
1/4 c. white wine

1 c. chicken broth
1 T. lemon juice
1 bay leaf
1/2 tsp. oregano
1 tsp. sugar
salt and pepper to taste
1-1/2 lb. white fish of choice

(more)

(continued)
Sauté garlic, onion, green pepper, mushrooms until browned. Add tomatoes, tomato paste, broth, wine, juice and seasonings. Cook until heated through. Add fish, which has been cut into large pieces and cook until it flakes easily, about 10 to 15 minutes.

Serve over spaghetti or rice.

CRAB LEGS WITH SHERRY BUTTER

2 lb. king crab legs   3 T. dry sherry
3 T. butter or margarine   2 T. lemon juice

Steam crab legs in a large stockpot for about 5 minutes, making 2 batches if necessary.

Sherry Butter:

Melt butter or margarine in a small saucepan, add sherry and lemon juice and simmer for 1 minute. Serve over the steamed crab.   75   **(more)**

(continued)

The crab can also be served cold with the hot sherry butter.

SALMON MOUSSE

1/2 lb. smoked salmon   pepper to taste
1/2 lb. cream cheese   1/2 tsp. ground cumin
1/3 c. green onions, chopped   Tabasco sauce to taste
1/4 c. dill   2 T. white wine
1/2 lemon, juiced

Put all ingredients in a food processor or blender and
blend to a fine puree. Spoon into a serving dish and
smooth the top. Chill thoroughly.

Serve cool with crispy bread slices.

SALMON WITH WINE SAUCE

2 lbs. salmon, 1/2" thick   1 clove garlic, chopped
salt and pepper to taste   1/4 c. olive oil
1 c. sherry   2 T. lemon juice

Put salmon in a baking dish and sprinkle with salt and pepper. Combine remaining ingredients and pour over fish. Bake at 400° for about 1/2 hour. *Do not overcook.* Pour pan drippings over fish when serving.

FRIED SHRIMP AND PEPPERS

1 lb. shrimp, uncooked
flour for dredging
2 T. Parmesan cheese,
1 tsp. salt

1 clove garlic, minced
4 green bell peppers,
   cut into thin strips
1/2 c. olive oil
1/4 c. white wine

Mix flour, Parmesan cheese and salt in a plastic bag.
Add cleaned shrimp and shake well to coat. Heat olive
oil in a skillet and add garlic and shrimp. Cover and

(more)

79

(continued)

cook about 5 minutes or until shrimp are golden.
Remove from pan and add pepper strips to skillet, cover
and cook for about 10 minutes, until tender.

Return shrimp to skillet with peppers. add wine and salt
and pepper to taste. Heat through.

SHRIMP FLORENTINE

2 pkgs. chopped spinach,   1-1/2 c. milk
   drained well   1/2 c. dry white wine
1-1/2 lb. shrimp, cooked   1/4 c. green onions chopped
1/4 c. butter or margarine   salt and pepper to taste
1/4 c. flour   1 c. cheddar cheese,
                                 shredded

Spread dried spinach in a 9" pie pan. Top with shrimp
and season to taste. In a saucepan, melt butter and stir
(more)

(continued)

(continued)

in flour. Gradually add milk, wine and green onions. Cook, stirring constantly until sauce thickens. Season to taste and add paprika until a rosy color. Pour over shrimp and sprinkle with cheese. Bake at 350° for 35 minutes.

This is best if made ahead and reheated

SHRIMP de JOHNGE

3 lbs. shrimp, uncooked   1 c. chicken broth
1 c. bread crumbs   2 cloves garlic, minced
1 c. sherry   1/2 lb. butter or margarine
1/2 c. parsley, chopped   salt and pepper to taste

Sauté shrimp in butter or margarine. Melt 1/2 lb. butter or margarine and combine with salt, garlic, parsley and bread crumbs. In a baking dish, alternate layers of shrimp and seasoned bread crumbs. Pour chicken broth and sherry over top and bake at 325° for 20 to 30 minutes, or until heated through.

SHRIMP NEWBURG

1 10-3/4 oz. can cream of shrimp soup

3/4 c. evaporated milk

1-1/2 c. shrimp. cooked

1/2 c. mushrooms, chopped

3 T. dry sherry

2 egg yolks, beaten

Put all ingredients, except egg yolks, in a crock pot and stir well. Cover and cook on low for 4 to 6 hours. Add the egg yolks at the last hour. Serve with rice or noodles.

Lobster or crab meat can be substituted.

CABBAGE ROLLS
(For Crockpot)

12 lg. cabbage leaves	1/2 c. red wine
1 lb. ground beef or lamb	salt and pepper to taste
1/2 c. cooked rice	1/4 tsp. thyme
2 8oz. cans tomato sauce	1/4 tsp. nutmeg
1/4 c. water	1/4 tsp. cinnamon

Wash and dry cabbage leaves. Put into microwave oven for about 20 seconds to soften.

(more)

85

(continued)
Combine ground meat, rice, salt, pepper, thyme, nutmeg and cinnamon. Put 2 T. meat mixture on each leaf and roll firmly.

Stack in crockpot. Combine tomato sauce, wine and water and pour over rolls. Cover and cook on low for 8 to 10 hours or on high 4 to 5.

FRUITY POT ROAST

3 to 4 lb. pot roast 3/4 c. burgundy
2 T. olive oil 1 clove garlic, minced
1/2 c. onion, finely chopped 1-3/4 c. dried fruit
1/3 c. carrot, finely chopped 3 T. flour

Brown meat in olive oil. Season with salt and pepper to taste. Add onion, carrot, wine and garlic and simmer over low heat for about 1-1/2 hours.

In the meantime, pour hot water over dried fruit and let

87 **(more)**

(continued)

stand for 1 hour. Drain and reserve liquid. put fruit on
meat and cook 45 minutes more. Remove meat and
fruit to a platter and add reserved fruit liquid to pan to
make 1-1/2 cups. Blend flour and water and stir into
liquid. Stir until thick and bubbly. Serve over sliced
pot roast.

SAVORY POT ROAST

1 boneless roast beef	1/4 c. red wine vinegar
1 lg. onion, chopped	2 tsp. salt
1 can cream of mushroom soup	1 tsp. Dijon mustard
	1 tsp. Worcestershire sauce
1 soup can water	1/2 c. red wine
3/4 c. brown sugar	

Brown beef and onion in a large pot. Combine all other

(more)

(continued)

ingredients except wine and pour over beef. Cover and simmer about 2-1/2 to 3 hours. Add more water if necessary. Add wine about 15 minutes before removing from pot. Let cool a little before slicing.

Serve with vegetable of choice and potatoes. Thicken gravy if desired.

SAUTÉED FILET TIPS

2 lbs. beef tenderloin tips	salt and pepper to taste
1/2 onion, chopped	Worcestershire sauce
1/4 green bell pepper, diced	Flour for thickening
4 beef bouillon cubes	Olive oil
1/4 c. red wine	

Sauté onions until translucent. Add peppers and beef and cook until beef reaches desired doneness. Add 1/2 c. water and the bouillon cubes.

(more)

(continued)
Bring to a simmer and add Worcestershire sauce to taste, red wine, salt and pepper. Bring to a boil and thicken with flour mixed with water.

Serve over noodles or rice.

SWEET AND SOUR BEEF STEW

1-1/2 lbs. beef stew meat,
   cubed
2 T. olive oil
2 med. carrots, shredded
2 med. onions, sliced thinly
1 8 oz. can tomato sauce
1/2 c. red wine

1/4 c. brown sugar
1/4 c. vinegar
1 T. Worcestershire sauce
salt to taste
1 T. cold water
2 tsp. cornstarch

In a large skillet, brown half the beef at a time in hot oil.

(more)

93

(continued)
Return all meat to pan and stir in carrots, onions,
tomato sauce, wine, brown sugar, vinegar,
Worcestershire sauce and salt.

Cover and cook over low heat about 1-1/2 hours or until
meat is tender. Blend 1 T. cold water with cornstarch
and add to stew. Cook until mixture is thickened.

This is tasty over hot noodles or rice.

SWISS STEAK

1-1/2 lb. steak, 1-1/2" thick	3 T. olive oil
flour	2 onions, sliced
salt and pepper to taste	1 lb. tomatoes, chopped
chile powder to taste	1/2 tsp. thyme
	1/2 c. red wine

Dredge steak in flour, chile powder, salt and pepper.
Brown in olive oil, remove from skillet. Add onions and
sauté until soft. Return meat to pan with the onions
and add tomatoes, thyme and wine.

(more)

(continued)
Cover and simmer for about 1-1/2 to 2 hours or until tender. Turn the meat occasionally. More wine can be added to thin the gravy.

BURGUNDY BURGERS

1-1/2 lb. ground beef   3 T. burgundy
2 T. olive oil   2 tsp. Italian spices
2 cloves garlic, minced   2 T. Dijon mustard
salt and pepper to taste

Mix all ingredients together and form 6 patties. Grill or cook to desired doneness.

Serve with grilled onions and tomatoes.

SAUERBRATEN MEATBALLS

meatballs
1 can beef broth
1/3 c. red wine

1/4 c. brown sugar
3 T. vinegar
1/3 c. gingersnaps,
  finely crushed

Heat broth and wine and 1/2 c. water and the balance of ingredients and bring to a boil. Put meatballs in sauce and simmer, uncovered, 20 minutes. Stir often to prevent sticking. *Good over hot buttered noodles or spatzel.*

98

BAKED HAM SLICE

1 ham slice, center cut, 1
   to 1-1/2" thick
1/4 c. onion, minced
1/2 c. white wine

2 med. oranges, peeled
   and cut into slices
1/4 c. brown sugar
1 med. lemon, sliced

Score ham fat to prevent curling and put into a baking
dish. sprinkle onion over ham. Arrange orange slices
on ham and sprinkle with brown sugar. Top with
lemon slices and pour wine over all.

(more)

(continued)
Refrigerate, covered, overnight. Bake at 375° until ham is tender, about 45 minutes.

GLAZED PORK CHOPS

2 T. olive oil
4 pork chops, 1/4" thick
1 lg. onion, thinly sliced
1/4 c. Worcestershire sauce

4 T. white wine
1 T. brown sugar
1/4 tsp. sage

Season chops and sauté in olive oil until almost done, about 8 minutes, turning once. Remove from skillet and add onion to pan and cook until golden brown, about 6 minutes. Stir in Worcestershire sauce, wine, brown

(more)

(continued)
sugar and sage. Bring to a boil. Continue cooking until
slightly reduced. Return chops to pan and simmer
uncovered about 2 minutes or until chops are done and
glazed.

CREAM SHERRY PORK TENDERLOIN

1 whole pork tenderloin	1 T. brown sugar
1 c. soy sauce	1/4 c. cream sherry

Combine soy sauce, brown sugar and cream sherry and marinate the pork tenderloin for 2 hours. Bake at 300° for 1 hour, basting often. Let cool slightly and slice thinly.

PLUMY PORK CUTLET

1 lb. pork cutlets, 1/2" thick 1/2 onion, chopped
1 T. olive oil   1/4 c. red wine
1 8 oz. jar plum jelly   2 tsp. soy sauce

Heat oil in a large skillet over medium heat. Brown
cutlets on both sides. Add remaining ingredients and
simmer, covered, 10-12 minutes.

CHIANTI CHICKEN

1 can cream of chicken soup 1/2 c. red wine of choice
1 pkg. onion soup mix   4 boneless chicken breasts,
                                     skinned

Combine soup and soup mix and wine and pour into a
baking dish. Top with chicken breasts and bake at 350°
for 1 hour or until chicken is tender.

Serve with a side of pasta.

CHICKEN BREASTS a la SHAREE

4 chicken breasts, skinless   4 slices bacon, halved
   and boneless   1 pkg. dried beef
1 can cream of chicken soup 4 T. milk
1/3 c. sherry

Line a casserole dish with dried beef. Put chicken
breasts, overlapping, on top. Cover with soup, wine
and milk, which has been mixed together. Lay bacon
slices on top and bake at 350° for 1-1/2 hours or until
tender.

106

CHICKEN SAUTÉED IN WINE

8 chicken breasts, boneless
   and skinless
4 T. olive oil
1 lb. mushrooms, chopped
12 green onions, chopped
1/2 c. dry white wine
1/2 c. light sherry

1/2 c. chicken broth
seasoned salt
garlic salt
salt and pepper to taste
flour for dredging

Dredge chicken breasts in flour and seasonings. Brown in olive oil. Remove and put into a baking dish. Brown

107

(more)

(continued)
mushrooms in drippings and place over chicken.

Add wine, sherry and broth to drippings and cook gently until thickened. Cook green onions for a few minutes in sauce. Pour over chicken. Cover and bake 1 hour at 350°. Sprinkle with chopped parsley before serving.

CHICKEN ROSEMARY

1 chicken, quartered
salt and pepper to taste
1 c. white wine

1-1/2 T. lemon juice
1 c. vegetable oil
1 T. rosemary

Put chicken into a baking dish. Sprinkle with salt,
pepper and add wine, oil and rosemary. Cover and
marinate in the refrigerator overnight. Drain chicken,
saving marinade. Broil or grill, turning frequently,
basting often. Cook until tender, about 30 minutes.

CHICKEN TETRAZINI

1 5 oz. pkg. thin spaghetti, cooked
4 c. cooked chicken
1/4 c. pimento
1/4 c. green or red pepper, chopped finely
1/4 c. onion, chopped
2 cans cream of mushroom soup
1/4 lb. cheddar cheese, grated
1/2 c. chicken broth
1/2 c. white wine
sautéed fresh mushrooms, if desired

Combine all ingredients and bake for 1 hour or microwave for 20 minutes.

CHICKEN ST. CLOUD

8 chicken breasts, boneless   1 can mushroom soup
8 slices prosciuto   1/2 pt. sour cream
8 slices Swiss cheese   fresh mushrooms, sliced
1/4 c. sherry
Combine soup, sour cream, wine and mushrooms. Put
chicken in a baking dish and cover with prosciuto slices.
Pour sauce over chicken, reserving some for later.
Bake, covered, 45 minutes to 1 hour at 350°. Cover
with cheese and the remaining sauce and bake an
additional 2 minutes, until the cheese melts.

GOLDEN CHICKEN

2 cans golden mushroom soup   8 chicken breasts,
3/4 c. dry white wine   boneless, skinless
2 pkg. dry onion soup

Mix mushroom soup and wine and pour over chicken in
a baking dish. Sprinkle with dry onion soup mix.
Cover and bake at 325° for about 1 hour or until tender
and no longer pink.

MUSHROOM CHICKEN WITH WINE

1 cut up chicken	1-1/2 c. chicken broth
1/4 . olive oil	1 bay leaf
4 T. green onions, chopped	1/4 tsp. rosemary
1/4 c. tomato paste	2 T. brandy
1/2 c. dry white wine	1 lb. mushrooms, sautéed
	salt and pepper to taste

Skin chicken and dredge in flour. Sauté in olive oil until golden. Remove chicken and sauté onions until

(more)

113

(continued)
tender. Add remaining ingredients and mix well.
Return chicken to pan and simmer, covered for about 1
hour. Add the sautéed mushrooms and heat until
warmed through. You may want to thicken the sauce.

Serve over noodles or rice.

SAUCY CHICKEN

2 T. butter or margarine
4 chicken boneless chicken
   breasts, skinned
1/2 c. onion, chopped
1/2 c. green pepper,
   chopped
1 c. mushrooms, sliced
1 pkg. golden onion soup

1-1/4 c. water
1/4 c. white wine
Worcestershire sauce to
   taste
1 T. cornstarch
3 T. water

Melt butter or margarine and brown chicken on both

(more)

(continued)

sides. Remove from skillet and reserve drippings. Add chopped onion, pepper and mushrooms and sauté until tender. Return chicken to pan.

Combine soup mix, water and Worcestershire sauce and pour over chicken. Cover and reduce heat. Simmer 20 minutes, adding wine about 10 minutes before finished.

Remove chicken to platter and combine cornstarch and water. Add to sauce to thicken. Serve gravy over chicken.

SOUR CREAM BAKED CHICKEN

6 chicken breasts, boneless
   and skinless
1 lb. mushrooms
flour for dredging

1/2 pt. sour cream
1/2 c. dry white wine
1/4 tsp. rosemary

Shake breasts in a plastic bag with flour until coated.
Brown each piece lightly in olive oil. Remove and
arrange in a covered baking dish.

In the same skillet, brown mushrooms lightly, then add

117

(more)

(continued)
sour cream, wine and rosemary. Simmer the sauce, *but don't boil*, until smooth. Pour over chicken and bake 1-1/2 hours at 300° or until tender.

The sauce should resemble a thin white sauce.

STUFFED CHICKEN BREASTS

6 T. butter or margarine.
1/4 c. onion, minced
1/2 lb. mushrooms, finely
    chopped
1 c. red wine

6 chicken breast halves
1 ea. red, yellow and green
    bell peppers, in strips
2 T. olive oil

In a skillet over medium heat, melt 3 T. butter or margarine and add onions, cooking until golden. Add mushrooms and 1/2 c. wine. Sauté on high until liquid has evaporated and mixture is dry.

119

(more)

(continued)
Put chicken in baking dish and tuck about 2 T. of mushroom mixture under the chicken breast. Melt remaining butter or margarine and the remaining wine and pour over chicken. Bake at 350° for 35 minutes or until tender. Baste occasionally.

Sauté pepper strips in oil and serve over the breasts.

TURKEY PICCATA

1/2 c. flour	2 T. butter or margarine
2 tsp. salt	2 T. olive oil
2 tsp. pepper	3 T. parsley
4 turkey cutlets, pounded thinly	lemon wedges

Combine flour, salt and pepper in a dish. Lightly flour cutlets on both sides. Heat butter or margarine and oil over medium heat, pan should be hot! Sauté cutlets for 2 minutes on each side. Remove from pan and cover.

(more)

(continued)
SAUCE INGREDIENTS:

1/2 c. dry white wine	4 T. capers, drained
1 lemon, juiced	salt and pepper to taste

Add wine to pan and cook, stirring constantly until
reduced to about 1/4 c. Remove from heat and add
lemon juice and capers. Season with salt and pepper to
taste. Pour over cutlets and sprinkle with parsley and
garnish with lemon wedges.

NOTES:

FRUIT AND SWEETS

FRUIT AND SWEETS

BURGUNDY PIE

1 lb. can sweet cherries,
   pitted
1 pkg. cherry gelatin
1 pt. vanilla ice cream

1 tsp. lemon juice
1/4 c. burgundy
1 9" pie shell, baked

Drain cherries, saving syrup. Add water to syrup to make 1 cup and heat to boiling. Dissolve gelatin in liquid and add ice cream a spoonful at a time, until melted. Stir in lemon juice and wine. Chill until mixture mounds. Chop cherries and fold into mixture. Chill again until firm.

126

APRICOT BLACKBERRY COMPOTE

2 ripe apricots
1/4 c. water
1/4 c. sugar

1/4 tsp. lime zest
1 c. dry white wine
1 c. fresh blackberries

Halve apricots lengthwise and pit. Cut each half into 4 wedges and transfer to a bowl.

Combine water and sugar and bring to a boil, stirring until sugar is dissolved. Stir in zest and wine and

(more)

(continued)
simmer 5 minutes. Pour over apricots and stir in
blackberries. Chill for 30 minutes.

Blueberries or other favorite berries can be substituted.

MELON ROSÉ SALAD

2 pkgs. orange Jello
1-1/3 c. boiling water
1/4 c. lemon juice
1/2 c. orange juice
2 tsp. orange zest. minced

1-1/2 c. rosé wine
3 c. melon balls, cantaloupe,
    watermelon, honeydew

Dissolve gelatin in boiling water. Cool and add all remaining ingredients except melon balls. Cool in refrigerator until thick enough that balls won't float.

(more)

(continued)
Add melons and pour into a ring mold. Refrigerate until set. Unmold and serve.

This is a very refreshing, pretty summer salad.

LEMON SHERBET

1 c. sugar
1 c. water
juice of 1 orange

juice of 2 lemons
2 c. dry white wine
1/2 c. whipping cream

Boil sugar and water for 4 to 5 minutes. Cool
completely then add the juices and wine. Put into the
freezer and when just about frozen, whip the cream and
fold in. Freeze again.

131

SHERRIED STRAWBERRIES

4 egg yolks	2 pts. strawberries, hulled
1 c. sugar	1/2 pt. whipping cream,
4 T. sherry	whipped

Combine egg yolks and sugar in a saucepan and cook until thickened, about 5 minutes. Remove from heat and add sherry, stirring well. Chill. When cool, fold whipped cream into the sherry mixture and chill again.

Slice strawberries in half and just before serving, fold into whipped cream mixture.

SHERRY CAKE

1 pkg. yellow cake mix   4 eggs
1 pkg. vanilla pudding   1 tsp. cinnamon
3/4 c. salad oil   1 tsp. vanilla
3/4 c. sherry

Mix all ingredients together and beat for 4 minutes.
Pour into a greased tube or bundt pan and bake at 350°
for 45 to 50 minutes. Sprinkle with powdered sugar.

This cake is best if made the day before.

133

BEVERAGES

134

BEVERAGES

SANGRIA

1/4 c. simple syrup
1 orange sliced thinly
ice cubes
1 qt. club soda

zest of 1 orange
1 T. lemon juice
1 bottle dry red wine,
   chilled

Put zest, slices, lemon juice and syrup in a pitcher and add wine and a few ice cubes. Stir well. Add club soda to taste, depending on how diluted you like your wine.

Serve in wine glasses.

CHAMPAGNE PUNCH

1/2 qt. pineapple juice	1/2 T. mulling spice
1/2 qt. grapefruit juice	1/4 c. sugar
1/2 qt. apple juice	1-1/2 qts. gingerale
1/2 can frozen lemon concentrate	1 bottle champagne

Put mulling spice in a tea ball or cheesecloth bag.
Combine first 6 ingredients and mix until sugar is

(more)

(continued)
dissolved. Chill for 12 hours to let the flavor of the spices come out. To serve, remove spices and add gingerale and champagne. Garnish with fresh fruit slices.

This will make about 35 4 oz. servings.

WHITE WINE SANGRIA

1/2 c. water	12 ice cubes or more
1 c. sugar	1 lemon, sliced thinly
1/4 tsp., cinnamon	1 orange, sliced thinly
2 bottles dry white wine	1 banana, sliced thinly

Combine water, sugar and cinnamon and bring to a simmer, cook 5 minutes. Put sliced fruit into a pitcher and pour hot syrup over them. Refrigerate until cold.

At serving time, add dry white wine, ice cubes and stir.

139   **(more)**

(continued)
For a different recipe, substitute dry red wine and add fruits in season, such as peaches, nectarines, strawberries, or blueberries.

NOTES:

SAUCES AND MARINADES

SAUCES AND MARINADES

143

BURGUNDY BARBECUE SAUCE

1 c. red burgundy	2 T. Worcestershire sauce
1 c. catsup	dash liquid smoke
1/2 c. cider vinegar	dash Tabasco sauce
1/2 c. water	1/2 tsp. dry mustard

Simmer all ingredients until onions are soft.

Pour over a beef or pork roast and cook until tender.

CHAMPAGNE BUTTER SAUCE

2 t. shallots, minced
1/4 c. champagne
2 T. chicken broth
2 T. lemon juice

2 T. heavy cream
1 stick unsalted butter,
    chilled
1 tsp. chives, chopped
salt to taste

Sauté shallots in 1 T. butter until soft, but not brown.
Add champagne, broth and lemon juice, simmer until
reduced by half, about 5 minutes. Reduce heat to low

(more)

(continued)
and stir in cream. Whisk in cold butter by tablespoons,
stirring constantly. *Do not add more butter until the
previous piece has melted completely.* Strain sauce
through a sieve and stir in chives. Salt to taste.

*This is so good over broiled or steamed salmon! Dry
white wine can be substituted for the champagne.*

BUTTERY WINE SAUCE

1 c. green onions, chopped 2 T. parsley, chopped
1 c. red wine   salt and pepper to taste
4 T. butter or margarine

Put onions and wine in a saucepan and bring to a boil.
Add remaining ingredients, stirring until butter is
melted. Serve warm.

Great served over chicken, fish or beef.

CHILI WINE SAUCE

1/2 c. chili sauce   1/4 c. dry red wine

Combine ingredients and serve at room temperature.

Good on burgers or chops.

CURRANT SAUCE

1/2 c. currant jelly   2 T. lemon juice
1/4 c. white wine   2 T. red onion, minced
salt and pepper to taste

In a small saucepan over high heat, combine jelly, wine, lemon juice and onion. Cook until jelly melts. Salt and pepper to taste.

Good over vegetables.

GRAPE WINE SAUCE

2 T. butter or margarine   2 lbs. white grapes,
2 T. olive oil   removed from the stems
1 c. white wine   1/2 c. half and half
                            salt to taste

Melt the butter then add the oil until heated through.
Add the wine and cover. Bring to a boil and reduce
heat and simmer for about 10 minutes. Add the grapes
and cook for 5 minutes longer. Add the cream and cook
for 2 minutes, stirring occasionally. Add salt if needed.
This is excellent over chicken or pork.

ITALIAN TOMATO SAUCE

2 c. tomatoes, peeled and   1/2 c. dry red wine
   chopped   1/2 c. black olives, chopped
1 can tomato paste   1/2 c. mushrooms, sliced

Combine all ingredients and blend well. Cook over
medium heat until it simmers. Reduce heat, cover and
simmer for 15 minutes to blend the flavors.

MINT SAUCE

1/4 c. butter or margarine   1/4 c. catsup
3/4 c. currant jelly   1 T. orange zest
1/4 c. fresh mint   1/4 c. red wine

Combine all ingredients and heat to blend flavors.
Store covered in the refrigerator.

Try this on lamb!

153

MORNAY SAUCE

3 T. butter or margarine   1-1/4 c. light cream
3 T. flour   1/4 c. dry white wine
1/2 tsp. salt   1/3 c. Swiss cheese,
1/8 tsp. nutmeg   shredded

Melt butter or margarine and blend in flour, salt and nutmeg. Add cream all at once. Cooking quickly, stir constantly. When mixture thickens, stir in wine and cheese and stir to melt.

Use instead of hollandaise sauce for eggs benedict.

MUSHROOM WINE SAUCE

1 c. fresh mushrooms	3/4 c. burgundy
1/4 c. green onions, chopped	3/4 c. water
1/4 c. butter or margarine	2 T. parsley
4 tsp. cornstarch	salt and pepper to taste

Sauté mushrooms and onions in butter or margarine until tender. Blend in cornstarch. Add wine, water, parsley and salt and pepper. Cook until bubbly. Serve over steak or chops.

155

ORANGEY WINE SAUCE

6 T. currant jelly
2 T. sugar
zest of 2 oranges
2 T. orange juice

2 T. lemon juice
2 T. port wine
salt and pepper to taste

Combine jelly, sugar and zest in a small bowl and whisk
until smooth. Add remaining ingredients and continue
whisking. Serve chilled.

ONION WINE SAUCE

3 T. butter or margarine   1/2 tsp. marjoram
4 lg. onions, finely chopped 1/4 tsp. ginger, ground
3 T. flour   1/4 tsp. nutmeg
1 tsp. sugar   1/2 tsp. thyme
1 10-1/2 oz. can beef broth 1 clove garlic, minced
1 c. red wine
1 T. tomato paste

In skillet, melt butter or margarine and add onions.

(more)

(continued)
Sauté over medium heat until browned. Stir in flour and sugar and stir until flour browns. Add broth and wine, stirring to combine flour. Add remaining ingredients and cook until blended, about 5 minutes.

Serve over steak or chops. Also good with poultry.

TOMATO SAUCE

2 lg. can crushed tomatoes	2 tsp. basil
5 cans tomato paste	2 tsp. garlic, minced
3 c. Roma tomatoes, chopped	5 bay leaves
	1 tsp. oregano
1-1/2 c. dry red wine	salt and pepper to taste
1 c. onion, chopped	

In a large pan, combine 3 c. water and all other ingredients. Boil over high heat, stirring often. Reduce heat, cover and simmer, stirring occasionally until

(more)

(continued)
**reduced to about 4 qts., about 1 hour. Remove bay
leaves.**

This can be used hot or cold.

WINE SAUCE

2 strips bacon, diced	1/4 tsp. thyme
2 tsp., shallots, minced	1 clove garlic, minced
1 T. butter or margarine	salt and pepper to taste
1 c. red wine	1 bay leaf
1 c. beef broth	1 T. flour
	2 T. butter or margarine, softened

Boil bacon for 3 minutes and drain. Sauté shallots in butter or margarine just until heated through. Add bacon, wine, broth, and spices. Cook over high heat

161 **(more)**

(continued)
until reduced to 1 cup, stirring often.

Combine butter and flour and whisk into wine mixture.
Return to heat and boil for 30 to 40 seconds, stirring.
Remove bay leaf. This is good with chicken or turkey
or even eggs at brunch.

TOMATO VEGETABLE SAUCE

1 c. onion, chopped	salt and pepper to taste
1 c. carrots, diced	1-1/2 c. milk
1 c. celery, diced	1 c. dry red wine
1/2 c. fennel, chopped	4 lb. tomatoes, chopped
2 T. garlic, minced	2 T. tomato paste
3/4 lb. ground beef	3 bay leaves
1/2 lb. ground pork	3 T. Italian seasoning

Heat olive oil in a large skillet and add vegetables.
Sauté until soft, about 15 minutes. Stir in garlic and

163

(more)

(continued)

cook another minute. Add the meats, breaking them up. Season and cook until meat is no longer pink.

Add milk and simmer gently until the liquid is almost evaporated. This will take a while so be patient. Stir often to prevent sticking. Add the wine and reduce until evaporated, about 20 minutes.

Add tomatoes, paste and seasonings, simmer over low heat for 3 to 4 hours until thick. Stir often.

(more)

(continued)
 Remove bay leaves and cool. Chill before serving.

Good on any pasta.

APPLE MARINADE FOR PORK

1/2 c. apple juice
6 T. soy sauce
1/4 c. honey
1 T. garlic, minced
1/4 c. red wine

1 T. ginger
1/2 T. dry mustard
1/4 tsp. Worcestershire
   sauce

Combine all ingredients together and mix well.

SWEET ONION MARMALADE

1/2 c. olive oil	1/4 c. red wine
6 sweet onions, thinly sliced	1/4 c. honey
6 cloves garlic, chopped	1/2 c. Parmesan cheese
1/2 c. pecans, chopped	grated
1/4 c. balsamic vinegar	3 T. rosemary
1/2 c. chicken broth	salt and pepper to taste

In saucepan over medium heat, heat oil. Sauté onions,

(more)

(continued)

garlic and pecans and cook until onions are tender and mixture is browned, about 30 minutes. Stir in broth, vinegar and wine and cook until reduced, about 10 minutes. Remove from heat and stir in honey, cheese, rosemary, salt and pepper. This can be covered and refrigerated for about 1 week.

Great on chicken or pork.

MUSHROOM VINAIGRETTE

2 T. olive oil

4 c. shittake mushrooms, trimmed and sliced

1/2 c. shallots, minced

1 c. white wine vinegar

1/4 c. dry sherry

2 T. sugar

salt to taste

2 T. Dijon mustard

1/2 c. vegetable oil

1/2 c. olive oil

2 tsp. thyme

pepper to taste

Divide mushrooms in half. Sauté in 2 batches in oil over high heat. Cook until lightly browned and most of the liquid is evaporated. Combine all mushrooms

(more)

(continued)
together when cooked and add shallots and garlic.
Sauté for 1-2 minutes, until tender.

Deglaze the pan with vinegar and sherry, scraping the
bottom of the pan to loosen any browned bits. Add
sugar and salt to taste. Reduce liquid by half. Stir in
mustard, then oils, thyme and pepper. Warm briefly
and remove from heat.

*This is good over cooked vegetables. Try it with
asparagus. Also good on chicken, pork or fish. Can also
be used with salad greens.*

RED ONION MARMALADE

2 red onions, halved and
   thinly sliced
2 c. rhubarb, thinly sliced
2 c. dried cranberries
1/2 c. dry red wine

1/2 c. brown sugar
1/3 c. red wine vinegar
1/4 c. honey
1/4 tsp. cinnamon
dash of salt

In a large saucepan, combine all ingredients and bring
to a boil. Reduce heat to medium and simmer and stir
for 20 minutes or until mixture is thick. Cool and serve
at room temperature.

ROQUEFORT DRESSING

1/3 c. green onions, chopped 1/2 lb. bleu cheese,
2 c. mayonnaise   crumbled
1 c. sour cream   2 cloves garlic, crushed
1/3 c. white wine vinegar 1/2 c. parsley, chopped
3 T. dry white wine   salt and pepper to taste
2 T. lemon juice

Combine all ingredients and whisk until thoroughly
blended.

NEED GIFTS?

Are you up a stump for some nice gifts for some nice people in your life? Here's a list of some of the best cookbooks in the western half of the Universe. Just check 'em off, stick a check in an envelope with this page, and we'll get your books off to you pronto. Oh, yes, add $2.00 for shipping and handling for the first book and then fifty cents more for each additional one. If you order over $30.00, forget the shipping and handling.

Mini Cookbooks

(Only 3 1/2 x 5) With Maxi Good Eatin' - 160 or 192 pages - $5.95

❑ Arizona Cooking
❑ Dakota Cooking
❑ Illinois Cooking
❑ Indiana Cooking
❑ Iowa Cookin'
❑ Kansas Cookin'
❑ Kentucky Cookin'
❑ Michigan Cooking
❑ Minnesota Cookin'
❑ Missouri Cookin'
❑ New Jersey Cooking
❑ New Mexico Cooking
❑ New York Cooking
❑ Ohio Cooking
❑ Pennsylvania Cooking
❑ Wisconsin Cooking
❑ Amish Mennonite Apple Cookbook
❑ Amish Mennonite Pumpkin Cookbook
❑ Amish & Mennonite
   Strawberry Cookbook
❑ Apples! Apples! Apples!
❑ Apples Galore
❑ Berries! Berries! Berries!
❑ Berries Galore!
❑ Bluberries Cookbook

❑ Cherries! Cherries! Cherries!
❑ Citrus! Citrus! Citrus!
❑ Cooking with Cider
❑ Cooking with Fresh Herbs
❑ Cooking with Spirits
❑ Cooking with Garlic
❑ Cooking with Things Go Baa
❑ Cooking with Things Go Cluck
❑ Cooking with Things Go Moo
❑ Cooking with Things Go Oink
❑ Cooking with Things Go Splash
❑ Crockpot Cookbook
❑ Good Cookin' From the
   Plain People
❑ Hill Country Cookin'
❑ Holiday Cookbook
❑ How to Make Salsa
❑ Kid Cookin'
❑ Kid Fun
❑ The Kid's Garden Fun Book
❑ Kid Money
❑ Kid Pumpkin Fun Book
❑ Midwest Small Town Cookin'
❑ Muffins Cookbook
❑ Nuts! Nuts! Nuts!

❑ Off To College Cookbook
❑ Peaches! Peaches! Peaches!
❑ Pumpkins! Pumpkins! Pumpkins!
❑ Some Like It Hot
❑ Squash Cookbook
❑ Super Simple Cookin'
❑ Working Girl Cookbook
❑ Veggie Talk Coloring &
   Story Book $6.95

In-Between Cookbooks

(5 1/2 x 8 1/2) - 150 pages - $9.95

❑ Amish Ladies Cookbook - Old
   Husbands
❑ Amish Ladies Cookbook - Young
   Husbands
❑ The Adaptable Apple Cookbook
❑ Bird Up! Pheasant Cookbook
❑ Breads! Breads! Breads!
❑ Camp Cookin'
❑ Civil War Cookin',
   Stories, 'n Such
❑ Cooking Ala Nude
❑ Cooking for a Crowd
❑ Country Cooking
   Recipes from my Amish Heritage
❑ The Cow Puncher's Cookbook
❑ Eating Ohio
❑ Farmers Market Cookbook
❑ Feast of Moons Indian Cookbook
❑ Fire Fighters Cookbook
❑ Football Mom's
❑ Halloween Fun Book
❑ Herbal Cookery

- ☐ Hunting in the Nude Cookbook
- ☐ Ice Cream Cookbook
- ☐ Indian Cooking Cookbook
- ☐ Little 'Ol Blue-Haired Church-Lady Cookbook
- ☐ Mad About Garlic
- ☐ Make the Play All-Sport Cookbook
- ☐ Motorcycler's Wild Critter Cookbook
- ☐ Outdoor Cooking for Outdoor Men
- ☐ Shhh Cookbook
- ☐ Soccer Mom's Cookbook

- ☐ Southwest Ghost Town Cookbook
- ☐ Turn of the Century Cooking
- ☐ Vegan Vegetarian Cookbook
- ☐ Venison Cookbook

Biggie Cookbooks
(5 1/2 x 8 1/2) - 200 plus pages - $11.95
- ☐ A Cookbook for them what Ain't Done a Whole lot of Cookin'
- ☐ Aphrodisiac Cooking
- ☐ Back to the Supper Table Cookbook
- ☐ Cooking for One (ok, Maybe two)

- ☐ Covered Bridges Cookbook
- ☐ Depression Times Cookbook
- ☐ Dial-a-Dream Cookbook
- ☐ Flat Out, Dirt Cheap Cookin'
- ☐ Hormone Helper Cookbook
- ☐ Real Men Cook on Sunday Cookbook
- ☐ The I-got-Funner-things-to do Cookbook
- ☐ Victorian Sunday Dinners

HEARTS 'N TUMMIES COOKBOOK CO.
1854 - 345th Avenue
Wever, Iowa 52658
1-800-571-BOOK

Name _____

Address _____

_____

*You Iowa folks gotta kick in another 6% for Sales Tax.